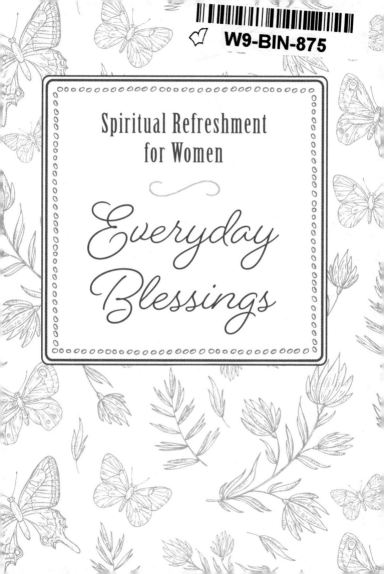

Spiritual Refreshment
for Women

Everyday

Blessings

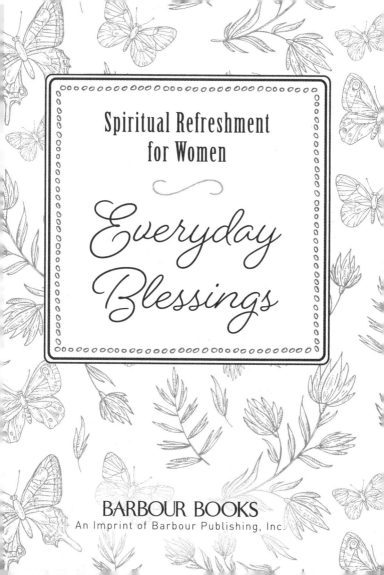

Spiritual Refreshment
for Women

Everyday
Blessings

BARBOUR BOOKS
An Imprint of Barbour Publishing, Inc.

© 2007 by Barbour Publishing, Inc.

Print ISBN 978-1-68322-480-8

eBook Editions:
Adobe Digital Edition (.epub) 978-1-62416-769-0
Kindle and MobiPocket Edition (.prc) 978-1-62416-768-3

Bible permissions can be found in the back of the book.

Writing and compilation: Rebecca Currington, Debbie Kubik Evert, Shanna Gregor, and Carol Smith in association with Snapdragon Group℠ Editorial Services.

Published by Barbour Books, an imprint of Barbour Publishing, Inc., P.O. Box 719, Uhrichsville, Ohio 44683, www.barbourbooks.com

Our mission is to publish and distribute inspirational products offering exceptional value and biblical encouragement to the masses.

ecpa Member of the
Evangelical Christian
Publishers Association

Printed in the United States of America.

Contents

Every good and perfect gift is from above, coming down from the Father of the heavenly lights, who does not change like shifting shadows.

JAMES 1:17

Introduction

Blessings are God's gifts to us—simple or great, they are produced by the overflow of His great love. We recognize these most often when they include a reprieve from sickness or a financial provision for a critical need. But we are prone to take for granted the sunshine that lights our days and lifts our spirits, the affection of friends and family, the kindness of strangers.

Everyday Blessings was created to open your eyes to the blessings all around you, to encourage you to bask in the loving-kindness of our awesome God. It is our prayer that as you move through these pages, you will see God's hand in every aspect of your life, filling it with goodness, hope, joy, and peace.

Abilities

We have different gifts,
according to the grace given us.

ROMANS 12:6

God has blessed every person—every single one—with some gift or ability with which to serve others and bring glory to His name. Some abilities are obvious—they shine brightly in front of everyone—but others move below the radar. They include things like the ability to pray effectively, love the unlovely, listen attentively. Ask God to open your eyes to your special abilities. They are God's blessings to you.

*Do not neglect your gift. . . . Be diligent in
these matters; give yourself wholly to them,
so that everyone may see your progress.*

1 TIMOTHY 4:14–15

⌒

The Bible most often refers to human abilities as gifts
because they are given in order to be given again. If you
have the gift of song, God expects you to strengthen and
polish that gift and use it to enrich the lives of others. If
you have been given a way with children, extend that gift
to every child you meet. As you use your gifts to bless
others, you will be blessed most of all.

Abundance

*Rejoice in the LORD your God, for he has
given you the autumn rains in righteousness.
He sends you abundant showers,
both autumn and spring rains.*

JOEL 2:23

As human beings, we are limited in what we can provide for those we love—our resources, both material and emotional, are finite. But God has no limits. He blesses His children far beyond our comprehension. He does more than just rain down His blessings on us; He sends abundant showers of blessing in every season of our lives. You are a rich woman. Once you see all God has provided for you, you won't ever want to come in out of the rain.

Grace and peace be yours
in abundance.

1 PETER 1:2

As you look around at God's blessings in your life, close your eyes and look inward, as well. God has also provided you with an abundance of grace and peace. Grace that allows you to be who you genuinely are and the peace of knowing that who you are is just fine with Him. Women are wonderfully emotional people, the keepers of the inner life. If your inner places are dark and empty, invite God to fill them to overflowing with His goodness.

Acceptance

*[God] chose us in Him before the foundation
of the world. . .according to the good pleasure of
His will, to the praise of the glory of His grace,
by which He made us accepted in the Beloved.*

EPHESIANS 1:4–6 NKJV

You may never receive the full acceptance and approval
of the people in your life. But God has already given you
His approval, His acceptance. He chose you. Think about
that. Almighty God chose you! No one compelled Him to.
His motive wasn't pity. The Bible says He created you and
pronounced His work "good." He's proud of the "you" He's
made, and He is moved with love for you—just as you are.

Honor God by accepting each other,
as Christ has accepted you.

ROMANS 15:7 CEV

Just as God has accepted you, He asks that you accept others. That doesn't mean you must accept their aberrant behaviors or keep your mouth shut when you see people doing things they shouldn't. Accepting others means appreciating that each person was created by and is loved by God. They have value for that reason. In loving Him, you must love whom He loves and accept whom He accepts. That's the only proper response to so great a Creator.

Accomplishment

A longing fulfilled is a tree of life.

PROVERBS 13:12

You are a fortunate woman! You live in a time when women can accomplish anything they set their minds to do. Are there still obstacles? Of course, but nothing you can't deal with. God has given you something special to do in this world. You'll know it by the longing you feel deep inside. Ask God to guide you, lending you His wisdom, grace, and strength. Then go for it. Nothing can compare with the joy of accomplishing God's will for your life.

Commit your work to the LORD,
and your plans will be established.

PROVERBS 16:3 NRSV

Whatever God has called you to accomplish in your life, He has not called you to accomplish alone. He is always there, providing you with the resources you need to get the job done. That doesn't mean you won't stumble along the way or encounter difficulties. But it does mean that you can call upon the counsel and resources of almighty God to help you. Whether you need wisdom, inspiration, confidence, strength, or just plain tenacity, you will find your answer in Him.

Stand firm. Let nothing move you.
Always give yourselves fully to the
work of the Lord, because you know
that your labor in the Lord is not in vain.

1 CORINTHIANS 15:58

⁓

Simply defined, *ambition* means determination to succeed. That's a positive thing—essential, in fact, to accomplishing God's will and purpose for your life. It helps you look past the obstacles in your path—age, health, education, lack of finances, etc.—to the prize waiting on the other side. God wants you to be determined, even ambitious. He's given you that inner motivation to help you complete the task He's assigned to you. Thank Him for it!

*Do nothing out of selfish ambition or vain conceit,
but in humility consider others better than yourselves.*

PHILIPPIANS 2:3

Ambition is a positive characteristic—unless it begins to take over your life. Are you pursuing your goals—even God-given goals—at the expense of others? Out of control, ambition can cause you to do things you would never do otherwise. God expects you to couple your ambition with godliness. Only then will you truly be accomplishing His will for you. Only then will you truly fulfill the desires He has placed in your heart.

Appearance

*What matters is not your outer appearance—
the styling of your hair, the jewelry you wear,
the cut of your clothes—but your inner
disposition. Cultivate inner beauty, the gentle,
gracious kind that God delights in.*

1 PETER 3:3–4 MSG

Most women care how they look. That's why they carry mirrors in their purses and purchase billions of dollars of makeup each year. There's nothing wrong with looking good on the outside as long as you remember to primp and preen your inner self, as well. God wants your beauty to be more than skin deep. He wants it to be heart deep. Work to be as fully beautiful as you were created to be.

*"The Lord does not look at the things man
looks at. Man looks at the outward
appearance, but the Lord looks at the heart."*

1 SAMUEL 16:7

When God looks at you, He sees a beautiful woman,
a temple worthy of His Spirit. He sees your virtuous life
and your godly attitudes. He sees a person whose heart
has been washed clean and fully submitted to His will and
purpose. He sees a beauty that is often missed by others.
He sees an inner beauty that transcends any physical characteristics—good or bad. God sees you as you really are.

Armor of God

Put on the full armor of God so that you can take your stand against the devil's schemes.

EPHESIANS 6:11

It's a good idea for every woman to take a basic class in self-defense in order to protect herself in this predator-filled world. A wise woman will learn how to defend herself spiritually, as well. God has provided you with a full suit of armor for that purpose—truth, righteousness, peace, faith, and salvation. Wear them everywhere you go. You do have an enemy, and he wants to take all you have. Be prepared to resist and defeat him.

Our struggle is not against flesh and blood,
but against the rulers, against the authorities,
against the powers of this dark world and against
the spiritual forces of evil in the heavenly realms.

EPHESIANS 6:12

In God's kingdom, women are called to be warriors. Alongside their Christian brothers, they are asked to battle with the forces of evil that plot to destroy human lives and keep them from knowing their Creator. This is a warfare fought in spiritual realms with an enemy we know is there but cannot see. Put on your spiritual armor and ask God to point out your battle station. And then—on to victory!

Assurance

When my skin sags and my bones get brittle,
GOD is rock-firm and faithful.

<small>PSALM 73:26 MSG</small>

It's the nature of a woman to need assurance—confirmation that she is pretty enough, smart enough, pleasing enough. God wants you to know that "you are more than enough!" He is pleased with you. He wants you to be assured that He will always be there for you. You need not fear that He will grow tired of you, lose interest, and abandon you. You are precious to Him, no matter your age, your condition, your circumstances. You matter to Him.

God affirms us, making us a sure thing in Christ,
putting his Yes within us. By his Spirit he has stamped
us with his eternal pledge—a sure beginning of
what he is destined to complete.
2 Corinthians 1:21–22 msg

The last time you bought a house or a car or applied for a loan, were you preapproved? Good feeling, isn't it? In a real sense, you have been preapproved for God's kingdom. He's given you His Word and stamped you with His eternal pledge. You belong to Him. He is fully committed to helping you become all you were created to be. You can turn your back on Him—it's true. But He will never turn His back on you.

Attitude

*Be constantly renewed in the spirit of your mind
[having a fresh mental and spiritual attitude].*

EPHESIANS 4:23 AMPC

Your attitude can substantially affect your happiness level. It's true. When your mind is assaulted every day by "stinkin' thinkin'"–things like, "I'm not good enough," "I'm not loved," "I'll never reach my dreams"–it's pretty tough to be happy. On the other hand, when you think about good things–God things–your happiness level will soar. Try it! "God loves me," "God is always by my side, watching out for me," "God has made me a winner." What a difference it will make.

Put off your old self, which is being corrupted by its deceitful desires; to be made new in the attitude of your minds; and to put on the new self, created to be like God in true righteousness and holiness.

EPHESIANS 4:22–24

The key to a great attitude is to rise above your old ways of thinking and start thinking like God thinks. The Bible says we aren't capable of thinking God's actual thoughts. They are too high and holy. But you can think like God—raising your mind-sight to focus on the good, the right, the holy, helping and encouraging others, and ways to express your thankfulness. An attitude is simply a response to what you see—keep your mind tuned in to the good.

Belief

He that cometh to God must believe that he is,
and that he is a rewarder of them
that diligently seek him.

HEBREWS 11:6 KJV

Belief is one of those things you can't see physically, but you still have it. For example, you believe a chair will hold you when you sit in it. You can't explain the physics of it, but you sit in it believing it will do what it's supposed to do. Belief in God is like that. You put your trust in Him that He will do what He said He would do. The Bible, His written Word, is filled with those promises.

*On the last and greatest day of the Feast,
Jesus stood and said in a loud voice,
"If anyone is thirsty, let him come to me
and drink. Whoever believes in me,
as the Scripture has said, streams of living
water will flow from within him."*

JOHN 7:37–38

Ever been so thirsty nothing can quench your thirst? You're desperate to find resolution. You try everything within reach. You even try substitutes, but they're just that: a substitution for the real thing. Sometimes we aren't just physically thirsty, but we have that deep-down soul-type thirst. You're seeking something in your life that will completely quench your parched soul. Jesus said that only He can satisfy that kind of thirst. He's there, no waiting. He can fill your life to overflowing.

Bible

Your word is a lamp to my feet
and a light for my path.
PSALM 119:105

⌘

If only life came with an instruction manual, you've said to yourself. Help for when you don't know what to do. The Bible is filled with stories of ordinary people who lived through struggles and triumphs, heartache and joy. Unlike the stories we see today on television, not every story has a happy ending. People saw consequences of their erroneous actions. Through it all, God shines a light for our paths today.

The word of God is living and active. Sharper than any double-edged sword, it penetrates even to dividing soul and spirit, joints and marrow; it judges the thoughts and attitudes of the heart.

HEBREWS 4:12

The Bible is God's love letter to you. It isn't the sappy romance novel found in drugstores. The characters in those stories give only conditional love to each other. God's love is unconditional. From the first words in the book of Genesis, where God created the heavens and the earth, He is communicating His love to you. It's the love letter you've longed to read. Open it up and see for yourself.

Burdens

*"Come to me all you who are weary
and burdened, and I will give you rest."*

MATTHEW 11:28

Weary. Burdened. Need rest. Those words read like a repeating entry in a woman's daily journal. Most women feel they've earned the right to be burdened. What else but weary could they be with all they have to do? Jesus said that He would give rest to those who are weary. He would lighten our loads. Take one burden at a time and hand it over to Him. And then rest in the peace that Jesus has our lives in the palm of His hands.

Carry each other's burdens, and in this
way you will fulfill the law of Christ.

GALATIANS 6:2

Have you seen the size of kids' backpacks lately? Their backs sway with the weight of books, papers, and "stuff." Kids carry these packs all day on their tired shoulders. Relief comes when they drop the weighty bags at home. The burdens you carry around each day may be causing your shoulders to droop, as well. Take those worries and burdens to God. He has promised to lighten your load by adding His shoulder to yours.

Challenge

Because the Sovereign LORD helps me, I will not be disgraced. Therefore have I set my face like flint, and I know I will not be put to shame.

ISAIAH 50:7

Life is full of challenges. While some are short-term, others last a lifetime. What keeps you determined and motivated? Do you seek the help of others or prefer to go it alone? Take a toddler's approach to these challenges. As she ventures into walking, she takes one step at a time, with help from a steady adult or an available piece of furniture. Eventually, she walks on her own. With God's help, take life's challenges one step at a time.

Let us run with endurance the race that is set
before us, looking unto Jesus, the author
and finisher of our faith.

HEBREWS 12:1–2 NKJV

Do you ever get tired of life's challenges? Do you wish you could live a carefree, predictable life? While that isn't possible, you can have a different perspective on the challenges that come your way. The Bible says we will encounter trials in this life. After all, this world is not our home; it's just a temporary residence. While we are here, though, God promised His presence, love, and comfort. He will walk beside you and give you strength to overcome whatever is in your path.

Change

*Jesus Christ is the same yesterday
and today and forever.*

HEBREWS 13:8 NASB

Your schedule fluctuates from day to day, and you have the calendar to prove it. Decades ago, life was pretty much the same every day, especially for women. Most of what we did was for others: church and big family dinners on Sundays, wash on Mondays, ironing on Tuesdays, etc. Aren't you glad you live in a time when you can experience new things every day? As you long for consistency, look to Jesus. His loving character never changes. He was, is, and will be.

If anyone is in Christ, he is a new creation;
the old has gone, the new has come!

2 Corinthians 5:17

The monarch butterfly begins life as a lowly worm. Through the course of time, it makes itself a cocoon and eventually turns into a beautiful butterfly. Similarly, we come to Christ with the potential to be a beautiful butterfly. Through challenges and normal life events, we go through a spiritual metamorphosis and become new creatures. We are free to fly and be what God intended us to be. His intention for you is beauty and grace. Trust Him to see you through the transformation.

Character

[The Lord] guides the humble in what
is right and teaches them his way.

PSALM 25:9

The phrase "We're known by the company we keep" is true regardless of whom you hang around with. It's also true when it's God you're spending time with. As you rest in His presence, read His words in the Bible, and talk to Him about all the issues of your life, you cannot help but take on some of His characteristics. He is peace, and you become more peaceful. He is good, and you take on His goodness. It's all about the company you keep.

We show we are servants of God
by our pure lives.

2 Corinthians 6:6 ncv

Character has been defined as what one is. It's the very essence of a person. The Bible says a lot about God's character and uses phrases such as "God is love"; "God is compassionate"; "God is merciful." His actions show His character. When we belong to God, we reflect His character: we are kind, loving, caring, compassionate. Our actions and behaviors reflect that character: we love, we care, we serve.

Charity

Happy are those who are
kind to the poor.

PROVERBS 14:21 NRSV

❧

You see people in need almost every day. Whether they are hungry or hurting, the Bible says to give out of the overflow of love you have received from God. He will work through you as you serve food to those who are hungry, give clothing to those who need covering, offer hope to those who feel hopeless. You can serve them with gentle words and kind deeds. Serving the powerless is a blessing in itself, but it carries a bonus—God's eternal reward.

"I tell you the truth, whatever you did
for one of the least of these brothers
of mine, you did for me."

MATTHEW 25:40

What would you do if Jesus came to your house for dinner? Although you might be nervous, He would want you to be yourself, to serve Him as you would any other guest. You would give Him the best you have, out of the abundance He has provided for you. It would not matter what was served, but He would delight in your efforts on His behalf. Jesus is pleased when you serve others as you would serve Him.

Children

If any of you lacks wisdom, he should ask God,
who gives generously to all without finding
fault, and it will be given to him.

JAMES 1:5

You can read books and ask others for advice as you raise your children, but how can you be assured what you're doing is the best for them? Just as your children come to you with questions, take your questions to God, your heavenly Father. No question is too small or too big. You can't stump Him, because He knows you and your children intimately. After all, He has created you all. God is the best resource you can find.

Children are a gift from God;
they are his reward.

PSALM 127:3 TLB

If you're a mother, you know how precious your children are to you. They are bone of your bone, flesh of your flesh. You would not hesitate to protect them with your life. And well you should, for that's your job. Take a moment to remember that you are God's child, created in His own image. He gave His very life to save you, and even now He hovers over you protectively. Your children are God's gift to you. You are God's gift to Himself.

Choices

"Choose life and not death!"
2 Kings 18:32

No matter how good—or bad—your choices have been in your life, there is really just one choice that matters. That is the choice of where you will spend eternity. God has given you a free will, and He expects you to use it. You must choose Him—consciously, intentionally choose Him—or you will be making a choice by default, a choice against Him. The Bible says it's a life-and-death matter. Your free will is His gift to you—use it!

"Choose this day whom you will serve. . .
but as for me and my household,
we will serve the Lord."

JOSHUA 24:15 NRSV

From the mundane to the life-altering, we make choices every day. Do you wish you could see into the future and know which direction your life will take if you make this or that choice? Perhaps it's for the best that we don't have that option. But you can put your trust in the One who does. Listen to the Lord; choose Him. When you do, it will be much easier to make the right choices for your life.

Comfort

The L<small>ORD</small> will hear your crying, and he will comfort you. When he hears you, he will help you.

I<small>SAIAH</small> 30:19 NCV

The Christian life is difficult—and emotional. It was for Jesus' disciples also. Jesus knew His death would be the most emotional moment of their lives. So just before Jesus gave His life on the cross, He sat down with them, explained that He would be leaving, and promised that He would send another "Comforter," the Holy Spirit. He has placed His Comforter inside of you. He hears every cry.

Whatsoever things were written aforetime were written for our learning, that we through patience and comfort of the scriptures might have hope.

ROMANS 15:4 KJV

God has given you another gift filled with His love and comfort—the holy scriptures. As you read about Noah, Abraham, Jacob, Joseph, Moses, Esther, Ruth, Job, David, Elijah, Mary, and Paul, you will see how God comforted them in their darkest hours. He will certainly do the same for you. Be encouraged as you read, and place your hope in His goodness. He will comfort you, and you can be sure of that.

Commitment

"Your hearts must be fully committed to the LORD our God, to live by his decrees and obey his commands, as at this time."

1 KINGS 8:61

Many women have issues with commitment. Their fear of failure causes them to drift in and out of relationships, jobs, and obligations without ever really settling anywhere. Committing your life first to God will help you commit later to others. Give Him your love, your life, your heart, and ask Him to help you walk out your commitment one day at a time. Everything else will follow.

Commit everything you do to the Lord.
PSALM 37:5 TLB

Some women can't commit, while others overcommit. Even when your intentions are good, you can bring down your whole house of cards by trying to juggle too many things—family, social events, work, spiritual time. Soon you find yourself with no personal time, becoming more stressed by the moment. Ask God to help you balance your commitments in a way that is healthy for you. Then you will be free to meet your commitments head-on and accomplish them with excellence.

Compassion

You, O Lord, are a compassionate and gracious God,
slow to anger, abounding in love and faithfulness.

PSALM 86:15

God never asks you to do anything for someone else that He has not already done for you. You are able to show compassion for others because He has shown compassion for you. When you were lost and lonely, He found you. When you were sick with sin, He forgave you. When your life was in shambles, He held you close and comforted you. When you longed for a fresh start, He opened the way before you. You give from what you have already received.

Never walk away from someone who deserves help;
your hand is God's hand for that person.

Proverbs 3:27 msg

The Bible reminds us that we are God's hands and feet. We carry His compassion to the world around us. What a wonderful privilege and responsibility. Ask God to open your eyes to the people around you who need His merciful touch, His gentle encouragement, His tender intervention. You won't be able to meet all the needs you see, but if you're asking, He will show you where you can make a difference. And when you raise another's head, you raise your own, as well.

Confidence

In quietness and in confidence
shall be your strength.
ISAIAH 30:15 KJV

Confidence is really just the quiet assurance that you are enough—enough of an employee to get the job done, enough of a wife and mother to take care of your family, enough of a woman of God to accomplish what He's called you to do. For some women, that comes easily, for others, not so much. If your confidence is lagging, reach out to God for help. He will help you unveil the real you—the confident and assured you.

Such confidence as this is ours through Christ before God. Not that we are competent in ourselves to claim anything for ourselves, but our competence comes from God.

2 Corinthians 3:4–5

As a child of God, you should be confident about who you are—not pushy or overbearing—a woman who knows she is the daughter of a great and mighty King. Draw your confidence from your relationship with your heavenly Father; then take life one challenge at a time. It isn't about being perfect. It's about being sure of whom you believe in and who you are in Him.

Contentment

I say it is better to be content with what little you
have. Otherwise, you will always be struggling
for more, and that is like chasing the wind.

ECCLESIASTES 4:6 NCV

When it comes to evaluating your life, God's scales weigh differently than yours. Seeing through His eyes, the smallest things can bring you the deepest joy. When you embrace your life just as it is, you can lay down the struggle for what might be or might have been. You can feel the blessing of contentment that, for this moment, your life is the perfect starting place for the next step in the journey.

I have learned to be content
with whatever I have.

PHILIPPIANS 4:11 NRSV

Having what you want, or wanting what you have. It's amazing what a difference the order of those simple words can make. What a gift it is to feel that sense of enough, to not always be thinking more, to believe that God has given what you truly need. As you focus today on the pockets of your life that you "wouldn't have any other way," whisper a prayer of thanks. Take a breath and let this moment be full, just on its own.

Courage

LORD, you are my shield,
my wonderful God who gives me courage.

PSALM 3:3 NCV

You never know where courage will pop up in your life, because you never know what you'll face that will require it. You can be sure, though, that God will give you courage when you need it. God is both your protector and your strength. So be confident that whatever you face, you do not face it alone. You face today with resources both from your own soul and the Spirit that dwells within you.

"In the world you have tribulation,
but take courage; I have overcome the world."

JOHN 16:33 NASB

While living in this world that you can touch and see, you must remember that you are also part of a world that can be known only through faith. In the physical world around you, you face disappointment and struggle, yes. But as a citizen of the kingdom of heaven, you are blessed with a greater power—someone who advocates for you. Jesus never claimed you would be without struggle, but He always reminds His followers of the victory that is waiting.

Daily Walk

Just as you received Christ Jesus as Lord,
continue to live in him, rooted and built up in him,
strengthened in the faith as you were taught,
and overflowing with thankfulness.

COLOSSIANS 2:6–7

Even though you don't always see progress in your walk with God, you can be sure that your roots are going down deep. Beneath the soil, God tends your faith—the longer you walk with Him, the deeper His hold on you. You came to Him with nothing and simply surrendered to His love. And that is all it takes—just a willingness to keep walking with Him and trusting that He's strengthening your roots beneath you.

Be very careful, then, how you live—
not as unwise but as wise.

Ephesians 5:15

As you walk with the Lord each day, you will face many crossroads. God will open the way before you, but He will not mandate your steps. He's given you a free will with which to choose the steps you take. He does admonish you to choose wisely, though. The safest way to do that is to keep your hand in God's hand at all times. He will never let you wander off the path. Reach out to Him and He'll be there.

Decisions

The human mind plans the way,
but the LORD directs the steps.

PROVERBS 16:9 NRSV

It's always good to have a plan. It's also good to acknowledge that plans change—and sometimes those detours actually lead us to a better way. Make your lists, set your priorities, perfect your agendas, and work them well. But in the midst of it all, remember to surrender them to God. Then sit back and watch what your willing and prepared heart can do in the light of His direction.

*"Who has known the mind of the Lord that he may
instruct him?" But we have the mind of Christ.*

1 CORINTHIANS 2:16

When you receive Christ, you are regenerated spiritually and given a renewed way of thinking. The Spirit of
God makes His home in you. You have the mind of Christ.
Given all that, shouldn't this life be easy? Shouldn't you
always know what to do? Not necessarily. You still have
your own nature and will, but you also have a resource to
turn to. As you quiet yourself and learn to hear the mind of
Christ within you, the way does become clearer.

Desires

The desires of the diligent are fully satisfied.

PROVERBS 13:4

It's a fact of life that you don't always get what you want. You've been learning that lesson since you were two and the floor wasn't too far away to stage a tantrum. But now that you are pretty far from the floor, you have to remember that there's a difference between having everything you want and being satisfied. God doesn't promise to fulfill your every craving, but if you live life in relationship to Him, you will be satisfied—fully satisfied.

Delight yourself in the L<small>ORD</small> and he will give
you the desires of your heart.

P<small>SALM</small> 37:4

What does your heart desire? How much of your mental space does that desire occupy? The teachings of the Bible address the irony of the desires of our hearts. When we focus our attention on God, good things come to us. Even those things we want the most. It's easy to think you should do the opposite—fight for what you want. The twist in the plot is that when you delight in God, your heart's desires are most easily met.

Determination

*"As for you, be strong and do not give up,
for your work will be rewarded."*

2 Chronicles 15:7

What is it that's threatening to make you lose your resolve and give up? Maybe it's exhaustion or discouragement. It might be niggling questions like, "Is this worth it? Is anyone going to notice?" The Bible promises over and over again that your determination will be rewarded. God sees even if no one else does. He understands the process and the difficulty. He will be waiting at the finish line, and your efforts in this life will be well worth it.

Let us hold fast the confession of our hope without wavering, for He who promised is faithful.

HEBREWS 10:23 NKJV

There's not a lot of faithfulness around these days. People make promises, but circumstances change. Life twists and turns. But God is faithful. The promises He's made, He'll keep. You don't always know how and when, and sometimes life can mislead you into thinking your hope is lost. But if you are determined to hold on, the fog will eventually clear and your course will become clear. God's counting on you to stay the course and never give up.

Love the LORD your God with all your heart
and with all your soul and with all your strength.

DEUTERONOMY 6:5

We talk about loving someone from the heart, but loving someone actually takes all of us. We don't just love God with our hearts. We love Him with our hearts, our souls, and our strength—we love Him with our whole selves. That's the kind of love He wants from you. You can lose your own self-focus in giving that kind of whole-self devotion, and losing your self-focus is what a surrendered life is all about.

*Guard my life, for I am devoted to you. You are my
God; save your servant who trusts in you.*

PSALM 86:2

Devotion to God comes with strings attached—or maybe
it would be better to say *promises*. When you give yourself
completely to God, you become an heir to eternal life, and
a child of His kingdom. Success is guaranteed in whatever
you do because you are carrying out His will. Give Him
every room in your heart. Open every door wide and invite
Him in. When He comes, He brings with Him peace, joy,
love, and much more.

Encouragement

You hear, O LORD, the desire of the afflicted;
you encourage them, and you listen to their cry.

PSALM 10:17

It's easy to feel unheard in this life. Even those closest to you may sometimes fail to listen. But God hears. He's never too tired, too busy, too distracted. You don't need an appointment. He's always listening, always encouraging. So cry out to Him. Share everything with Him—those things that cause you pain, those things that bring you joy. Let Him in on your secrets and your hopes. He will never fail you.

*Think of ways to motivate one another
to acts of love and good works.*

HEBREWS 10:24 NLT

The great thing about Christian community is that we inspire each other in this Christian walk. Haven't you caught someone red-handed in some kind of faithful act and felt inspired? And who knows how many times your faith has been spotted and someone made a better choice "next time" because they saw the choice you made? That's the wonder of rubbing elbows in the fray together. Faith alone strengthens you. But faith together inspires more faith!

Eternal Life

"God so loved the world that he gave his one and only Son, that whoever believes in him shall not perish but have eternal life."

JOHN 3:16

Life here on earth is fleeting. One day we are sitting on the floor playing with our favorite dolls, and then we find ourselves a grown-up woman dealing with grown-up issues. In what seems like a moment, we notice gray hair and wrinkles tickling the borders of our youthful faces. Life happens, and that's why God created a way for us to live on, free from time and age. Through His Son, He bought eternal life for you. What greater gift could there be?

*"My sheep listen to my voice; I know them,
and they follow me. I give them eternal life,
and they will never die, and no one
can steal them out of my hand."*

JOHN 10:27–28 NCV

In eternity, we will have no need of protection. All will be well as we occupy the heavenly kingdom. But here on earth, there are many hazards. God has not left your eternal life to chance. He purchased it for you with the sacrifice of His own Son. Then, He Himself watches over you so that nothing and no one can keep you from reaching your destination. The life God has given you is not up for the taking. It is sealed by His promise.

Example

Be an example to the believers with your words,
your actions, your love, your faith,
and your pure life.

1 TIMOTHY 4:12 NCV

‿‿

Setting an example for others can seem like a heavy weight—always having to watch your words and your actions. Being good on your own is a simple impossibility. There's only one way that you can live worthy to represent God. That is by letting Him live through you. When your self-interest crowds to the forefront, surrender yourself to Him. Soon you will find yourself demonstrating for others that it's possible to live a pure and godly life.

*Provide people with a glimpse of good living
and of the living God.*

PHILIPPIANS 2:15 MSG

Have you ever heard someone say, "Your actions are talking so loud that I can't hear what you're saying"? It's true—people pay much more attention to what you do than what you say. That's why the way you live as a child of God is crucial. Those who would dismiss you as a religious fanatic when you try to talk to them about your relationship with your Creator will be unable to ignore your exemplary life. Let them see Jesus in you.

Expectations

In the morning, O LORD, you hear my voice;
in the morning I lay my requests before
you and wait in expectation.

PSALM 5:3

It takes a lot of faith to hope. Even more to expect. But you can do both when it comes to your faith and your prayers. It's not that you will always pray for a specific thing and get it, like placing a catalog order online (not that that always works out either). But what you can expect, when you lay your concerns before God, is that He will answer. Your prayers do not fall on disregarding ears. You can count on that.

*"Be ready all the time. For I, the Messiah,
will come when least expected."*

LUKE 12:40 TLB

Jesus promised His return, and He asked that His followers watch for Him. He hasn't told us when—only that it will be when the world least expects Him. Only those who are sensitive to His Holy Spirit will recognize the times and the seasons. He expects you to live with the certainty that He will return soon and to live your life accordingly. What a glorious day that will be. Look for it! Expect it!

Faith

*Keep alert, stand firm in your faith, be courageous,
be strong. Let all that you do be done in love.*

1 Corinthians 16:13–14 NRSV

Faith is not something you commit to once then don't think about again. Instead it's something that alerts you every day to possibilities and opportunities. God has called you to live a life of vibrant faith, open to His direction, keeping your eyes on Him. Day by day you will see His faithfulness and your faith will grow. Soon you will stop worrying about what is around the next corner. You'll know with certainty that the two of you can handle any eventuality.

We live by faith, not by sight.

2 CORINTHIANS 5:7

You've probably heard it before—seeing is not believing; believing is seeing. It's more than a twist on a phrase. Your faith opens you up to a new awareness of life around you. It enables you to see more from God's point of view. It reminds you that life is not just about the everyday realities but also mystery and possibilities. When you believe, you live according to a whole other reality with sights and sounds unimaginable to faithless eyes.

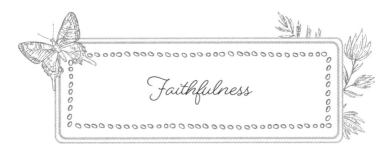

Faithfulness

The faithful will abound with blessings.

PROVERBS 28:20 NRSV

We've all had tasks that looked easy at the onset but later threatened to scuttle our resolve. We wonder if it's worth it to hang on. But when we do, we find that the reward of the task accomplished is even sweeter. Are you wondering if you can finish the task God has assigned to you? Don't give up. Your faithfulness to God's purposes holds the promise of great reward. Ask God to help you faithfully carry on until the job is done.

Your love, O LORD, reaches to the heavens,
your faithfulness to the skies.

PSALM 36:5

God won't abandon you. He won't walk away. His faithfulness reaches farther than you can see or even imagine. It's difficult to take in that kind of faithfulness when you live in a world full of disappointments. But if you can get quiet enough inside to sense God's never-changing presence and His steadfast commitment to you, you can survive the disappointments of this life so much more bravely. His faithfulness never fails!

Family

All thy children shall be taught of the LORD;
and great shall be the peace of thy children.

ISAIAH 54:13 KJV

There's no heritage like the knowledge of God's love. There's no inheritance as empowering. As you live your life of faith before your family, it's like stocking a vault that will bless everyone. And it's never too late to begin. As you live authentically before God, you leave a blueprint for those who are watching. That example can last for generations, beyond your view, more influential than you can fathom.

A wise woman strengthens her family.

PROVERBS 14:1 NCV

The influence of a woman on her family is phenomenal—for good and for bad. Sadly, some women weaken their families through selfishness, ambition, and carelessness. The vigilant, wise, and godly woman holds her family together, makes sacrifices to ensure its stability, and entreats God's blessing with her prayers. You can be that kind of woman—the kind that builds up and strengthens. Ask God to help you. He will show you how.

Feelings

We can be sure when we say, "I will not be afraid, because the Lord is my helper."

HEBREWS 13:6 NCV

Women are complex beings. Our emotions are our greatest strength, but they can also be the most unstable aspect of our character. How do you respond to the pressures and pleasures around you each day? Do you find yourself too emotional? God doesn't want to stifle your emotions—they allow you to feel His love, His compassion, His joy. Instead, He wants to help you harness them and use them for His kingdom. Will you let Him?

*When times are good, be happy; but when times
are bad, consider: God has made
the one as well as the other.*

ECCLESIASTES 7:14

You may tend to think of God gratefully in the good times and ask for His help in the bad. But sometimes you have to consider that God brings good out of both. No matter what your feelings tell you, you can trust Him to work out His purpose in you at all times. He isn't bound by your feelings. He is bound by His Word. You should not be bound by your feelings, either, but by His promises!

Fellowship

*If we are living in the light of God's presence,
just as Christ does, then we have wonderful
fellowship and joy with each other.*

1 JOHN 1:7 TLB

⌒

Living in close relationship with God empowers you
to connect with people meaningfully. As you grow toward
Him, you will find yourself growing in your relationships
with others, as well. It's the result of having the same heavenly Father, living in the same kingdom, and sharing the
same destination—heaven. Enjoy the great spiritual family
God has placed you in. It's the family of faith. Be there for
them and let them be there for you. It's what God intended.

*All of you should be in agreement, understanding
each other, loving each other as family,
being kind and humble.*

1 PETER 3:8 NCV

The family of God is in many respects like your natural family. You love them profoundly, but very often they can make you throw up your hands in frustration. Just like you, they all have those little areas where they are still growing and learning and becoming better people. When conflicts come, don't turn and run! It's important to work it out and see it through—for your Father's sake.

Finances

Wealth hastily gotten will dwindle,
but those who gather little by little will increase it.
PROVERBS 13:11 NRSV

In a world where people win lotteries and game shows to suddenly come into a lot of cash, it's easy to wonder if it's worth it to put that little bit into savings each paycheck. The Bible says a lot about money, though, and affirms that it is the wise person who builds that nest egg as they can, a little at a time along the way. Besides the investment, that bit you put away, no matter how small, is a vote for your future.

My God will meet all your needs according to his glorious riches in Christ Jesus.

PHILIPPIANS 4:19

It may seem strange to learn that God cares about money. While He isn't subject to it, He knows that you are—while you live in this world at least. The Bible provides good advice about staying out of debt, saving all you can, being generous with others, and giving to the support of God's work. These habits put you in line for God's blessings. He describes them as "running over" and invites you to test Him and see.

Forgiveness

I forgive you all that you have done,
says the Lord GOD.
EZEKIEL 16:63 NRSV

You are forgiven. No matter what you've done. No matter how or when or what—God's forgiveness is waiting for you. The moment you acknowledge your sin and ask to be forgiven, it's done. Strangely, that may be difficult for you to accept. You may feel you must make your own atonement. But it's a feat you will never accomplish. Only God's perfect Son was able to do the job. Abandon your pride and receive His forgiveness. Don't wait another moment.

*Bear with one another and, if anyone has a complaint
against another, forgive each other; just as the Lord
has forgiven you, so you also must forgive.*

COLOSSIANS 3:13 NRSV

If you've ever tried to forgive another person, even a close friend or family member, you know how difficult that can be. Everything in you wants to cling to the hurt and publish the offense. God invites you to forgive out of gratitude for what He's done for you. He has forgiven you—freely and completely. Remember that no one could hurt you as much as your sin has hurt your heavenly Father. When you look at it that way, forgiveness becomes a privilege.

Freedom

The Lord sets prisoners free.

Psalm 146:7

Some women run from God, thinking He will ask them to surrender their freedom and lock them down to some religious regimen. In reality, just the opposite is true. We are all already in bondage to our unwashed thoughts and behaviors and our sinful nature. Before you can flourish in God's kingdom, He has to remove your bonds. Fortunately, your heavenly Father is in the chain-breaking business. Ask Him to set you free.

The Lord is the Spirit, and where the
Spirit of the Lord is, there is freedom.

2 CORINTHIANS 3:17

Wherever the Spirit of God goes, freedom follows. If His Spirit dwells in you, you will experience more freedom than you have ever known. You will no longer be inhibited by selfishness and resentment. You will be free to do what you were created to do—live in right relationship with your Creator. Don't struggle to free yourself. You haven't the power or the strength. Invite God's Holy Spirit to come inside your heart and free you in the process.

Fresh Start

"I will give you a new heart
and put a new spirit within you."
EZEKIEL 36:26 NKJV

Some of the most surprising news about God's presence is that He does more than fix you up the best He can and send you on your way—somehow He makes you brand-new. His offer of new life is one of the few truly fresh starts you can experience. Sure, He doesn't delete the consequences that still have to be battled through—but He does have the power to change your heart and help you manage those consequences. Ask Him to make you new!

You have begun to live the new life, in which you
are being made new and are becoming
like the One who made you.

COLOSSIANS 3:10 NCV

God's work in your life doesn't simply make you a better person; it makes you more like Him! That's really true of any loving relationship—the more you focus on another person and interact with him or her, the more you pick up that person's habits and interests. In the same way—but even more because of the work of the Spirit—as you focus on God and interact with Him, His nature is recovered in your life.

Friendship

A friend loves at all times.
They are there to help when trouble comes.

PROVERBS 17:17 NIrV

~

Tough times reveal real friends. Partly that is true because real friends are the ones that stick around when things are troublesome and uncomfortable and not at all fun. But also it is true because when you are at your worst or weakest, you can only bear to be witnessed by real friends—those who already know you inside and out and accept you just the way you are. Ask God to give you that kind of friend.

Some friends play at friendship but a true friend sticks closer than one's nearest kin.

PROVERBS 18:24 NRSV

It's nice to have acquaintances. But somewhere within us, we crave authentic friendships that provide a connection as strong as that of our biological families. Do you have friendships that reach to this level? If not, ask God to help you find the ones that you can go deeper with. Then keep your eyes and ears open. Reach out to others, and let God do the rest. He won't disappoint you.

Fruitfulness

"Abide in me as I abide in you. Just as the branch cannot bear fruit by itself unless it abides in the vine, neither can you unless you abide in me."

JOHN 15:4 NRSV

You may think you aren't accomplishing anything in your life. Perhaps you work at a dead-end job or a disability has left you feeling useless and alone. No matter what your circumstances, God has a plan for you, and that plan is not out of reach. As long as you are looking to Him, your life will be fruitful and fulfilling. That's His will, His promise, and His plan.

*"You did not choose me, but I chose you and
appointed you to go and bear fruit—
fruit that will last."*

JOHN 15:16

⌒

Have you looked at yourself and thought, *God could
never use me*? You've just decided that you aren't worthy
to go out in His name, to speak on His behalf, to carry
His message, to fulfill His plan. If it were up to you, you
wouldn't appoint yourself to do anything. But it isn't up
to you. God does the choosing, and He wants to use you.
He's given you a job to do. Open your heart and mind to
Him, and much fruit will follow.

Future

I know the plans I have for you, says the Lord,
plans for your welfare and not for harm,
to give you a future with hope.

JEREMIAH 29:11 NRSV

Your age doesn't matter. Your looks don't matter. Your circumstances don't matter. For every individual, every life, God has a plan for the future. Even if you are reading this book from a hospital bed from which you never expect to leave, God has given you a future. Don't drop out of life for any reason. With Him, your best days are yet to come—better than you can think or imagine.

Good people can look forward to a bright future.

PROVERBS 13:9 NCV

When your life is hidden in the goodness of God, your possibilities are limitless. Your future is more than bright—it's dazzling. If you are at the beginning of your walk with God, you are a fortunate woman. The road ahead may not be easy, but it will be the greatest adventure, the greatest race you've ever attempted. And best of all, the destination is certain. Throw yourself unreservedly into the work that God has called you to. Take hold of your future with both hands.

Gentleness

*"Take my yoke upon you and learn from me,
for I am gentle and humble in heart,
and you will find rest for your souls."*

MATTHEW 11:29

God could blast you for your sinfulness. He could reprimand you every time you stumble and chastise you for every mistake you make. He will correct you, of course. How else can He keep you on the right path? But God's correction is consistently gentle. No throwing of lightning bolts and crashing thunderclaps, just a still, small voice inside your heart. He will not make an excuse for your sin, but He will quietly and gently call you to repentance.

Let your gentleness be evident to all.
The Lord is near.

<small>PHILIPPIANS 4:5</small>

The Bible says that the *strong* woman is also *gentle*—two
words that might seem contradictory. But they aren't. The
strong woman chooses how she will respond to others. She
chooses to deal with them gently—because she can. She is in
control of her emotions, her words, and her actions. Anger,
hostility—both represent the easy way out. But gentleness
requires strength. God wants to see you become a strong,
gentle woman for Him.

Goodness

When wisdom enters your heart, and knowledge is
pleasant to your soul. . . you may walk
in the way of goodness.

PROVERBS 2:10, 20 NKJV

When you were a little girl, your parents may have said, "Run along now and be a good little girl." They meant only the best, but growing up, many women received a negative message. They relate goodness to being dismissed or not being taken seriously. Others become obsessed with meeting an unrealistic standard of goodness. Really, no one is good but God. Goodness will come as you walk in relationship with Him.

*As we have opportunity, let us do good
to all people, especially to those who
belong to the family of believers.*

GALATIANS 6:10

*G*ood deeds are an expression of the goodness or "God-ness" that resides within you. They should come easily, naturally. As you feel God's presence within and see Him moving in your affairs, as you feel your heart flooding with gratitude for what He has done for you, reach out to others. Let them feel the overflow of God's goodness to you. Good deeds aren't something you force yourself to do. They are the joyous privilege of the child of God.

Grace

By the grace of God I am what I am, and his grace
to me was not without effect. No, I worked harder
than all of them—yet not I, but the grace
of God that was with me.

1 CORINTHIANS 15:10

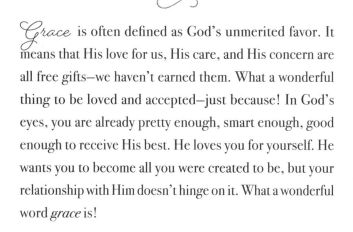

Grace is often defined as God's unmerited favor. It means that His love for us, His care, and His concern are all free gifts—we haven't earned them. What a wonderful thing to be loved and accepted—just because! In God's eyes, you are already pretty enough, smart enough, good enough to receive His best. He loves you for yourself. He wants you to become all you were created to be, but your relationship with Him doesn't hinge on it. What a wonderful word *grace* is!

[God] gives grace to the humble.

PROVERBS 3:34

For many people, it's difficult to receive what they don't feel they have earned. Whether it's a sense of independence or pride, such an attitude will rob you of the best this life has to offer. You must be able to receive God's love, even when you don't feel lovable, and God's goodness, even when you don't feel deserving. God has freely given you everything–His kingdom! Don't stand on the sidelines whispering, "I'm not worthy." Humble yourself and receive.

Guidance

Your ears shall hear a word behind you, saying,
"This is the way, walk in it," whenever you turn
to the right hand or whenever you turn to the left.

ISAIAH 30:21 NKJV

When we need answers, we often say we are "seeking God." And yet, we need not seek Him since He is ever near. Nor are we seeking answers from God, for He has already given us the answers we need. Instead, we are seeking to hear those answers, to tune out the busy thoughts and pre-conceived notions we carry with us. If you need answers, ask God to help you listen and discern, to open your ears to hear His voice that was there all along.

I will instruct you and teach you in the way you
should go; I will guide you with My eye.

PSALM 32:8 NKJV

Have you been asking God for guidance, but the way
before you is still unclear? It could be that you're expecting
a full-blown road map—and God rarely answers that way.
Instead, He gives the first step, and when you have taken
that step, He reveals the next. That's how He encourages
your faith and keeps you close to the path. It's enough really
to know that He sees the path ahead. Trust Him!

Happiness

A happy heart makes the face cheerful,
but heartache crushes the spirit.

PROVERBS 15:13

Happiness is elusive in this life. Because it's an emotion—like sadness and anger—it comes and goes with the circumstances. Joy is different. It's the permanent condition of the heart that is right with God. It isn't based on circumstances, but rather the known outcome—eternity with God. Forget about the pursuit of happiness and embrace joy. It will not fail you even in your darkest days and most trying hours. Rejoice!

May the righteous be glad and rejoice before God;
may they be happy and joyful.

PSALM 68:3

Many women believe that happiness is a result of success. "When I find the right person to marry, I'll be happy." "When I achieve my career goals. . ." "When I can afford the home I really want. . ." The truth is that real happiness—deep inner joy—is the result of living in right relationship with God rather than the trappings of success. Regardless of what you may be facing—good and bad—be happy knowing you are pleasing your heavenly Father.

Help

God is our refuge and strength,
an ever-present help in trouble.

PSALM 46:1

Have you ever gone through a trial or heartache so painful that you couldn't even put it into words? It felt like a long, piercing scream was ripping you apart inside. Any number of things could cause such suffering—loss, divorce, betrayal, sickness. If you find yourself in such a place in your life, reach out to the Lord. He understands suffering at its deepest level. He knows how to comfort you. All you have to do is ask.

Our soul waits for the LORD;
He is our help and our shield.

PSALM 33:20 NKJV

Whom do you turn to when trouble comes your way? You're blessed if you have faithful friends and loved ones here on earth. But whether you have such support in your life or not, God has promised you will never face adversity alone. Again and again in the Bible, He declares His desire to help you. Even when no one else is there—He will be. And He has limitless resources. No matter what your need, call on Him.

Hope

*The LORD is good to those who hope
in him, to those who seek him.*

LAMENTATIONS 3:25 NCV

Hope is amazing. It can grow and thrive even in the bleakest circumstances. A prisoner of war suffers brutal abuse at the hands of his captors, but they cannot break his spirit or rob him of the hope that one day he will be free again. It's hope that keeps us moving forward, always looking for a better day. Hope is God's gift. Thank Him for it by placing your hope in Him. He is profoundly faithful.

Why are you downcast, O my soul? Why so disturbed within me? Put your hope in God, for I will yet praise him, my Savior and my God.

Psalm 42:5–6

People hope in many things—money, possessions, other people, power, fame, and status, even their own strength. None of those things have the power to sustain hope. But God does. Money and possessions can be gone in a moment, but He will never change. People will fail you, but He will never let you down. Power, fame, and status are remarkably fragile. Even your own strength will one day be gone. But God will still be by your side. Place your hope in Him.

Hospitality

Do not forget to do good and to share with others,
for with such sacrifices God is pleased.

HEBREWS 13:16

The true meaning of hospitality is opening up your heart to others, making them feel at home in your presence. That means you can be hospitable anywhere you are. It doesn't require a fancy house or a gourmet meal. When you reach out to someone else with love and acceptance, you have shown that person hospitality. Look around you. Ask God to show you those people whom you can minister to just by opening your heart.

*Do not neglect to show hospitality to strangers,
for by this some have entertained
angels without knowing it.*

HEBREWS 13:2 NASB

It's easy enough to show hospitality to your family and friends, but God asks that you reach out to strangers, as well. That takes courage. But God is pleased when you look past your own shyness and hesitation to touch the life of a person you don't know. Instead of focusing on how it makes you feel, think about how it could affect a stranger—alone in a crowd. Your hospitality has the power to change a life for eternity.

Humility

With humility comes wisdom.

PROVERBS 11:2 NLT

The Bible says that Jesus is the only begotten Son of God, ruling and reigning with His Father from their heavenly throne room. And yet, He did the unthinkable. He chose to be born as a baby, live as one of us, and then suffer reproach and abuse, finally death. He humbled Himself and allowed Himself to be placed on the cross—for you. His humility accomplished the plan of salvation. Imagine what your humble obedience to His will can accomplish.

By humility and the fear of the LORD are riches,
and honour, and life.

PROVERBS 22:4 KJV

If you think being humble will make you a doormat for others to walk on and take advantage of, you couldn't be more wrong. Many associate humility with weakness, but it is more closely defined as strength. It takes no special effort to behave proudly. Pride comes naturally to human beings. But humility—that's not so easy. It means making a choice to do the difficult thing, the God thing. Submit yourself to God and reap the benefits of humility.

Integrity

*"I know, my God, that you test the heart and are
pleased with integrity. All these things have
I given willingly and with honest intent."*

1 CHRONICLES 29:17

Do you have a secret, something you are keeping hidden deep within, something that causes you to live in shame? You shouldn't think that you are keeping anything from God. He sees your heart. He knows all about you. And He wants to free you from the burden you are carrying. Confess your secret sins to Him—those you've committed and those committed against you. He will wash your heart clean. Then He will praise you as you live honestly and openly before Him.

Whoever walks in integrity walks securely.

PROVERBS 10:9 NRSV

Choosing to do the right thing in a situation may be difficult, even painful. It could mean the loss of income, a broken relationship, or an embarrassing confrontation. But whatever it takes, keeping your integrity is vitally important. When you do what is right, you preserve your soul. You'll make mistakes—no doubt about that—but God is there to forgive you and help you stay on track in the future. When you choose integrity, you choose the Lord.

Justice

Don't insist on getting even; that's not for you to do.
"I'll do the judging," says God. "I'll take care of it."
ROMANS 12:19 MSG

Many times when we are mistreated, we respond with vengeful thoughts and actions, forgetting that we look to a higher court—the authority of God. It isn't easy to lay down your offense, especially when your heart is aching for justice, but when you do, God is able to act on your behalf. Seeking revenge keeps you in a cycle of reciprocal hurt. Laying your grievance before God's high court frees you to move on. Trust God's pure justice and let Him fight your battles.

The LORD loves the just and will not forsake his faithful ones. They will be protected forever.

PSALM 37:28

Often we cry for justice when we have been wronged but not when we have wronged others. God wants us to care about both—because He does. Be sure that in all your transactions you require a high standard of fairness from yourself. Ask God to point out your blind spots so that your heart might remain pure before Him. When you mess up, be quick to make things right. God will be watching—and applauding.

Kindness

When the kindness and love of God our Savior
appeared, he saved us, not because of righteous
things we had done, but because of his mercy.

TITUS 3:4–5

Do you find it easy to offer kindness to those you feel deserve it—but not to those who don't? That's a normal human response. But when you begin to understand the fullness of God's kindness to you personally, you're apt to see things in a different light. You weren't deserving or even grateful, and yet He was kind to you. He held nothing back. Being kind to those who don't deserve it is a powerful way to demonstrate your likeness to your heavenly Father.

Who can find a virtuous woman? for her price is far above rubies. . . . She openeth her mouth with wisdom; and in her tongue is the law of kindness.

PROVERBS 31:10, 26 KJV

Kindness is often misunderstood. It doesn't mean stepping back and letting others dictate to you. And it doesn't mean coddling and indulging others. It means being gentle, friendly, benevolent, and generous with another person, especially when there is no expectation of receiving anything from that person in return. You won't have to go looking for opportunities to be kind; they will appear on their own dozens of times a day. Be like your heavenly Father—be kind!

Leadership

"The greatest among you must become like the youngest, and the leader like one who serves."
LUKE 22:26 NRSV

Not everyone is called to be a leader, but if you feel God's call and sense you have been given the attributes you need to lead others, you are right to step out from the crowd and make it known. Just know that leadership in God's kingdom is a position of service. Like Moses and King David and Paul the apostle, God will humble you before He uses you. But if you're willing and obedient, He may use you to change the world.

Be ye followers of me,
even as I also am of Christ.

1 CORINTHIANS 11:1 KJV

In order to be a good leader in God's kingdom, you must be a good follower—not of others, but of God. You aren't charged with setting the pace or cutting the path before you, but of keeping your eyes on the Lord and following His every move. That means you must know the principles He's laid out in the scriptures and live in close and constant relationship with God. It's a big responsibility to lead others, and a great privilege.

Learning

Let the wise listen
and add to their learning.

PROVERBS 1:5

Being a Christian is all about being a student in the things of God. What a wonderful blessing! Each day you are charged with getting to know your heavenly Father better and becoming more like Him. That will sometimes be painful as you discard old thought patterns and behaviors in favor of new ones, but it will always be productive, transforming you into the person God created you to be. Stay close to Him, listen, and learn all you can.

Teach the righteous and
they will gain in learning.

PROVERBS 9:9 NRSV

The number one characteristic of the unrighteous is their inability to learn. They make the same mistakes over and over, never recognizing their error or understanding that they have been given the power to change. You have seen the error of your ways and turned to God. Now continue to learn, continue to change, and continue to grow in the image of your heavenly Father. He is proud of your progress in righteousness.

Life

The way you tell me to live is always right;
help me understand it so I can live to the fullest.

PSALM 119:144 MSG

God has given us guidelines to live by—principles laid out in amazing detail in the Bible. Some say His rules are simply designed to bolster His ego. That's the same lie the devil told Eve when he tempted her to disobey God in the garden of Eden. "He's just trying to keep you from having something good," he taunted. Like any good parent, God has given us rules to ensure our safety and success. Living His way is always for your best.

*"I have come that they may have life,
and have it to the full."*

JOHN 10:10

$\mathcal{A}$ baby spends nine months in its mother's womb becoming the person God has created it to be. In comparison to its life lived outside the womb, this preparation time is amazingly short. In the same way, our lives here on earth are relatively brief and intended as a time to grow and prepare for eternity with God. You are being groomed for eternal life. That will truly be living to the fullest measure.

Loneliness

I am convinced that. . .neither the present nor the
future, nor any powers, neither height nor depth,
nor anything else in all creation, will be able
to separate us from the love of God
that is in Christ Jesus our Lord.

ROMANS 8:38–39

You don't have to be alone to feel lonely. It's all about how you are connecting with those around you. Perhaps you are in a place in your life where you feel no one understands you and no one cares. This time in your life probably won't last long. You will make connections and the loneliness will pass, but until it does, remember that God has promised to always be there for you—to listen, to comfort, to encourage. He's as close as your prayer.

God sets the lonely in families, he leads forth
the prisoners with singing.

PSALM 68:6

It isn't God's will for you to feel alone or lonely. He has gone to great lengths to include you in His family and surround you with spiritual brothers and sisters. Open your heart and let God help you make connections with His people. You will find that Christian fellowship goes deeper than any relationships you have had. It has permanence and variety. God wants to send your loneliness packing. Let Him set you squarely in His family.

*From everlasting to everlasting the LORD's
love is with those who fear him, and his
righteousness with their children's children.*

PSALM 103:17

God loves you! It's not complicated or conditional—it's just a fact! Our human understanding can't comprehend the reason why, only that it's true. As much as you might want to explain it, dissect it, reason it out, you just can't. Instead of wrapping yourself in questions, wrap yourself in His love. Luxuriate in it just as you would a magnificent fur coat. God has spared no expense. He has given you the very best He has to offer.

"A new command I give you: Love one another.
As I have loved you, so you must love one another.
By this all men will know that you are my
disciples, if you love one another."

JOHN 13:34–35

God loves you relentlessly, completely, and in spite of your flaws and shortcomings. His greatest desire is for you to love in the same way. He asks you first of all to love Him in return and then to love others. When you love, you show that you are His child; you demonstrate who you are and what you're made of. That pleases your heavenly Father more than any great work you might do on His behalf. Live to please Him by loving others.

Marriage

Let marriage be held in honor by all.

HEBREWS 13:4 NRSV

Since God placed the first man and woman in the garden of Eden, He has endorsed and blessed marriage. Except for those who have been set apart—like the apostle Paul—for singleness, God uses marriage as a tool to purify us. Through it He teaches lessons on faithfulness, trust, love, humility, service, gentleness, and much more. It is His refining fire. All the more reason to set your heart to live and grow within the boundaries of this holy union.

Your Maker is your husband—
the LORD Almighty is his name.

ISAIAH 54:5

Women find themselves single all the time. Some are single by their own choice or as part of God's plan for their lives. Others may be divorced or widowed. If you are single for whatever reason, you may be surprised to learn that you are in a highly favored position. The Lord says that He is the one who will provide for you and defend you. You can look to Him for love and companionship. He's more faithful and wise than any human husband.

Nature

God's glory is on tour in the skies,
God-craft on exhibit across the horizon.

PSALM 19:1 MSG

Look outside right now; better yet, go outside. Daytime or nighttime, it doesn't matter. Just look around you. If you live in a concrete jungle, look up at the sky. Imagine for a moment the immensity of God's creation, the grandeur of it. And yet, He calls mankind His most splendid creation—all the rest was called into being only to benefit His human creation. God values you above all else. Look up at the sky and consider that.

"Walk out into the fields and look at the wildflowers."
MATTHEW 6:28 MSG

Our God cares about details. You see it throughout His creation. Every species unique and every creature unique within its species. Human beings, created in His image and yet each one of a kind. Flowers and trees awash with color and refinement, even those growing along the highway, sown as it were by the wind. When you wonder if God is interested in the details of your life, consider the evidence demonstrated in nature. He cares about everything—no matter how inconsequential.

Patience

Patience is better than strength.

PROVERBS 16:32 NCV

Our electronic world does not encourage patience. Internet providers tout newer, faster technologies. What used to take days, even weeks, can now be done in minutes. Not everything can be rushed, though. God still does things in His own way and His own timing. He won't be bullied or hurried. He wants to strengthen and test your faith. When you feel impatient waiting for God to move on your behalf, resolve to trust Him. Surrender yourself to Him. You can be sure that He knows best.

Be still before the L<small>ORD</small>,
and wait patiently for him.

P<small>SALM</small> 37:7 <small>NRSV</small>

⌘

*D*o you remember as a child waiting for Christmas morning or to open your presents on your birthday? "Just wait. It will all happen in due time," your mother would say. God won't withhold from you just to be cruel or make a point, but He does see the big picture, and He knows the right when, where, and how. So don't get anxious, just wait. You will see what God has promised you—all in due time.

Peace

You, LORD, give true peace to those who
depend on you, because they trust you.

ISAIAH 26:3 NCV

Peace is to the kingdom of God what oxygen is to the atmosphere. Considering this truth, you may be wondering why you so often feel agitated and anxious. Think of it this way. Though oxygen permeates the air around us, we must breathe it into our lungs for it to do us any good. You must choose to let God rule in your heart. You must invite Him in. As you open your heart to Him, the peace will follow.

Let the peace of Christ rule in your hearts,
since as members of one body
you were called to peace.

<small>COLOSSIANS 3:15</small>

God often uses peace as a way of giving His children guidance. When you are praying about an important decision or life choice, you should pay close attention to the amount of peace you have concerning it. In any case, you should not move when your peace is replaced by a sense of anxiety or unrest. Move back in the other direction until the peace returns. You will never go wrong as long as you follow the peace.

Power

[God] gives strength to the weary
and increases the power of the weak.

ISAIAH 40:29

In the time of Jesus, widows and orphans were the most disadvantaged members of society. They were essentially powerless in a culture where women were not valued except through their husbands. These disenfranchised women are often mentioned in the New Testament, however. Jesus made it clear that they were to be treated kindly, with respect, and taken care of. He raised them from their less-than-nothing status to full acceptance in the body of believers. You are never powerless when you belong to Him.

[Be] strengthened with all power according
to his glorious might so that you may
have great endurance and patience.

COLOSSIANS 1:11

There aren't enough hours in the day to do a woman's work. No wonder we often feel exhausted and unhappy. The Bible says that there is a remedy for our endless activity. He strengthens us, empowering us to push through and get our jobs done. Sometimes He does that by empowering us to say no when we should, rest when we should, and keep our lives balanced. Ask Him for a transfusion for your life.

Praise

*Ye are a chosen generation, a royal priesthood, an
holy nation, a peculiar people; that ye should shew
forth the praises of [God] who hath called you
out of darkness into his marvellous light.*

1 PETER 2:9 KJV

Your life is a song of praise that rises to God your Father. He revels in your decision to take His hand and step out of darkness into light. It's what He has worked so hard to accomplish. It's why He sent His Son, Jesus, to live and die and rise again. You are His trophy, His prize, the sure and certain reward of His great sacrifice. Each time you say yes to life, yes to love, yes to eternal values, you are praising Him.

I will praise You, O LORD, with my whole heart. . . .
I will sing praise to Your name, O Most High.

PSALM 9:1–2 NKJV

Your life is a form of praise, but your words of praise are
even more precious to your heavenly Father. His Holy Spirit
who lives within you carries them straight to His throne.
Why are your praises so dear to Him? Because, unlike His
other creatures, your praises are not innate. They are the
free expression of your heart. You chose Him when you
could have chosen so many others. Lift your voice to Him.
It brings Him great joy.

Prayer

Pray and ask God for everything
you need, always giving thanks.

PHILIPPIANS 4:6 NCV

Prayer is quite simply conversation with God. What a joyous privilege we have to be able to speak to Him—almighty God—whenever we desire. How could you ever get enough of those times with Him? Meet with Him often to talk about your life. Tell Him your troubles and leave your worries at His feet. Confess your sins to Him and receive His forgiveness. Tell Him how much you love Him and how grateful you are to be His daughter. He's always ready to listen.

When you call upon me and come and pray to me,
I will hear you. When you search for me, you will
find me; if you seek me with all your heart.

JEREMIAH 29:12–13 NRSV

Is there a great need in your life? Something you have struggled with and can't seem to find the answer for? God says to bring it to Him—not just once, but again and again. Keep asking. Keep reminding Him of His promises. Like a child who campaigns for a new bike, never give up. Seek God and keep on seeking Him. He hears you each and every time, and He will reward your persistence and your patience after He proves your heart.

Presence of God

Blessed are those who have learned to acclaim you,
who walk in the light of your presence, O Lord.

PSALM 89:15

Close your eyes and imagine yourself sitting on the beach, a warm breeze tickling your skin and the comforting sound of waves breaking on the shore. Or think of yourself in a garden, the sounds of songbirds and enchanting fragrances in every direction. Place yourself anywhere, but know that nothing can compare to being in the presence of God. The treasures of the universe are stored there, His love surrounds you, and peace flows like a beautiful river. Come and enjoy.

"Where two or three come together in my name, there am I with them."

MATTHEW 18:20

God loves to be where His people are. His Holy Spirit dwells in each one of them, but when believers come near each other, something heavenly happens—not only does He dwell in them, but He also fills the distance between them. In this atmosphere, the impossible becomes possible and love becomes manifest. God urges you to meet together with other believers regularly. He knows what can happen when you do.

Fear God and keep his commandments,
for this is the whole duty of man.

ECCLESIASTES 12:13

God knows how busy your life is. As you move from task to task, remember to hold on to the golden cord that connects you to Him. He's always there regardless, but the cord reminds you that He is. It keeps the conversation going between the two of you, and His love, joy, and peace flowing to you throughout your day. God should be your first priority because it is through His wisdom and strength that you accomplish the others.

150

Seek those things which are above, where Christ is,
sitting at the right hand of God. Set your mind
on things above, not on things on the earth.

COLOSSIANS 3:1–2 NKJV

Human beings can be hopelessly shortsighted. But the person who sees past today and plans for eternity has both the present and the future in mind. When you accepted Christ's sacrifice for you on the cross and asked God to forgive your sins, your future in heaven was sealed. But the Bible also talks about laying up treasure in heaven. Place your priorities on those things that are eternal rather than those things that are just for this world alone.

Protection

The LORD your God will lead you
and protect you on every side.
Isaiah 52:12 GNT

We all have fears—fear of harm, fear of losing a child, fear of being alone, fear of failure. When your fears rise up and threaten to overcome you, when you feel sick in the pit of your stomach and your heart aches with anxiety—remember this. God is with you, every day, every hour, every moment. Focus on Him, really focus, and you will see that your fears are nothing more than speculation that is swept away in His presence.

The Lord watches over all who love him.

PSALM 145:20

Like any loving parent, your heavenly Father keeps you in His constant care, never letting you out of His sight. You have no reason to fear, for He is always with you, ready to face whatever comes your way. He will not fail you. In some cases, He will warn you ahead of time. In others, He will supernaturally remove you from a dangerous situation. And there will be times when He will hold your hand as you walk through fire. He is your God!

Provision

God will generously provide all you need.
Then you will always have everything you
need and plenty left over to share with others.

2 CORINTHIANS 9:8 NLT

God has promised to take care of you, but it doesn't stop there. He wants to provide for you abundantly—so much that you can share it with others. His provision isn't limited to money. He is the provider of all you need. If you need joy, He'll give it to you with enough to share. If you need wisdom, it's there for you, as well. Whatever you have on your list—ask Him for it. Then trust Him.

"Your Father knows what you need
before you ask him."

Matthew 6:8

God wants you to have everything you need for a great life. But sometimes we pray and things don't happen when we expect them to. You must trust that His timing is perfect. None of us live in a vacuum. Sometimes your request requires compliance on the part of other people, and they may not be prompt to respond. Don't give up. God will answer your prayer in the perfect way at the perfect time.

Relationships

Be devoted to one another
in brotherly love. Honor one
another above yourselves.

ROMANS 12:10

Jesus' ultimate sacrifice—laying down His life so that all humanity could experience eternal life—showed true devotion. His willingness to go to the cross gave you the opportunity to experience an intimacy with God that was not available before. Likewise you can honor others with the same love. That strength and power of love resides within you. God gave you the ability to show His love to everyone you meet. Be bold! Be courageous! Love like Jesus does! It's in you!

Kinsfolk are born to share adversity.

PROVERBS 17:17 NRSV

Your family holds a powerful place in your life. The same is true of your sisters and brothers in the Lord. They know your greatest strengths and most intimate weaknesses—but with a different agenda. The family of God is to build you up in the area of your weakness and draw from you in the area of your strengths. Though often painful, this is a process designed to make you strong and fruitful. There is great reward in enduring the adversity of relationships.

Renewal

Create in me a pure heart, O God,
and renew a steadfast spirit within me.

PSALM 51:10

No two snowflakes are alike. No two sunsets are ever exactly the same. Your Creator delivers a masterpiece with every stroke of artistry He inspires. You are no different. With each touch of His hand, with every letter you read in His Word, He changes your heart from old to new—forming you in His image. You become more like Him each moment you spend with Him. Your Creator makes all things new—and He's continually shaping the perfect you!

Though outwardly we are wasting away,
yet inwardly we are being renewed day by day.

2 Corinthians 4:16

Your relationship with God is alive. It's living and breathing and requires nourishment to survive. Much like tributaries pour into lakes and rivers, you give out of your spirit into all you do. When you give out, you can drain your reserves. God wants you full. Fill up as you renew your spirit and mind daily with His Word and in His presence. You're a life-giving river of living water. Fill up, pour out, and fill up again!

Respect

A kindhearted woman gains respect.

PROVERBS 11:16

As you grow in God, you begin to demonstrate His character and nature in your thoughts, attitudes, and behavior. Through you, His goodness becomes evident to others, and their respect for you increases. This will happen not because you demand it but because it is a natural response to God's glory. For the same reason, you must respect yourself—casting down thoughts of inferiority and unworthiness. Respect God's presence and work within you.

Knowledge begins with respect for the LORD.

PROVERBS 1:7 NCV

The Hebrews who walked across the Red Sea had such a reverence for God that they never said His name out loud. They had great respect for Him. Though your relationship with God is much different today, He still desires your respect. You are His child and He adores you. You are privileged to show Him your admiration. Give Him respect through praise, worship, and adoration. He wants to hear you—His precious child—say His name!

Responsibility

Whatever you do, work at it with all your heart,
as working for the Lord, not for men, since you know
that you will receive an inheritance from the Lord as
a reward. It is the Lord Christ you are serving.

COLOSSIANS 3:23–24

Sometimes it may feel like your hard work goes unnoticed. Maybe you're tempted to slack off like the other guy, telling yourself that no one will ever know. God knows your heart. The One that holds the future in His hands sees your faithfulness. He has entrusted you with much responsibility because He knows He can count on you. He will reward you and will bring you into a place of blessing. Expect it and believe He'll do it. God applauds you!

There are different kinds of service,
but the same Lord.

1 Corinthians 12:5

You may feel the weight of responsibilities you have been given. God made your shoulders broad enough to carry all that has been assigned to you. Embrace your responsibility knowing God has given you grace to carry it—and when it seems too heavy, He's always there to help you. He won't leave you alone to do what He's asked you to do. He won't let you fall under the weight. He won't condemn you for stumbling under the load. He's there for you!

Rest

The beloved of the LORD rests in safety—the High God
surrounds him all day long—the beloved
rests between his shoulders.

DEUTERONOMY 33:12 NRSV

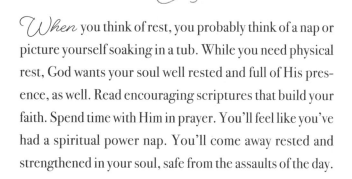

When you think of rest, you probably think of a nap or picture yourself soaking in a tub. While you need physical rest, God wants your soul well rested and full of His presence, as well. Read encouraging scriptures that build your faith. Spend time with Him in prayer. You'll feel like you've had a spiritual power nap. You'll come away rested and strengthened in your soul, safe from the assaults of the day.

On the seventh day God. . .rested from all his work.

GENESIS 2:2 NLT

Many women put in forty hours a week at a full-time job and then come home to care for the house and family. Don't forget to take time out for you. If God rested after working all week, then it's important to take care of yourself. The list of things to do will wait. Press the PAUSE button and rest your mind, body, and emotions. You're precious and valuable to God and all of those who love you. You're worth it. Take a moment and relax.

Reward

You know that the Lord will reward everyone for whatever good he does.

EPHESIANS 6:8

Have you ever received a reward for an act of kindness? Maybe you returned a wallet or found a lost pet. So often the goodness of God goes unnoticed. He gives with open hands never expecting anything in return because His motivation is love. He loved you enough to give up everything. You can give something to God. Become the rewarder! Let Him know that His grace and mercy have not gone unnoticed. Reward Him with your praise and thanksgiving.

The LORD recompense thy work,
and a full reward be given thee.

RUTH 2:12 KJV

Perhaps you feel unappreciated for the things you do for others—the cooking, cleaning, a late night at the office. Just once a thank-you would be reward enough. Someone does take notice of all you do. Your heavenly Father is watching even when it seems no one notices. He's proud of you and appreciates all you do. You show the love and life of God to those around you. Take heart—God is your exceedingly great reward.

Righteousness

The work of righteousness shall be peace;
and the effect of righteousness
quietness and assurance for ever.

Isaiah 32:17 kjv

What a comfort it is to know that God has paid the price for all your mistakes and declared you righteous based on the life of His own flawless Son. When the enemy comes to condemn you, the blood of Jesus stands between you and anything the devil accuses you of. Jesus paid the price and God found you righteous—without blame. Rest assured that God is on your side. You've been cleared of any wrongdoing by the highest court. You're right in God's eyes.

The path of the righteous is like the first gleam of dawn, shining ever brighter till the full light of day.

PROVERBS 4:18

God knows where you're going. As you journey on the road toward God's purpose and plan for your life, the light of God's love grows brighter with each step, bringing you closer and closer to Him. The more you know Him, the more quickly you know His will and His ways and can more assuredly step out in faith toward His righteous cause. Your steps are sure because your path is well lit with the goodness of God. You're on the right path.

Sacrifice

The sacrifices of God are a broken spirit;
a broken and contrite heart, O God,
you will not despise.

PSALM 51:17

No matter where you've been, God loves you. He doesn't care about your past but instead wants to give you an awesome future. You were worth the ultimate sacrifice. God gave all He had for you—at the highest cost. He cherishes you more than anything. You are the high prize that His Son, Jesus, was willing to fight and die for in order to restore you to your heavenly Father. Give Him your brokenness. It's a sacrifice you can afford to make.

*I urge you. . .in view of God's mercy, to offer your
bodies as living sacrifices, holy and pleasing to
God—this is your spiritual act of worship.*

ROMANS 12:1

You are the greatest house ever built. The King of kings desired to take up residence in you. Just like you'd expect a palace to be well cared for, so you should take care of your own body. Choosing to live a pure and holy life brings honor and glory to Him. Your character and behavior testify of His residence much like the lawn of a palace speaks of the royal family and their stature. Rejoice! You are the temple of the Most High God.

Salvation

*[God] says, "In the time of my favor I heard you,
and in the day of salvation I helped you."
I tell you, now is the time of God's favor,
now is the day of salvation.*

2 CORINTHIANS 6:2

Jesus' death on the cross was God's plan to bring you into heaven once your time on earth is through. But God had much more in mind than you might imagine. Jesus' death, burial, and resurrection offer freedom from any bondage you face. God doesn't want you to miss a single blessing. Let Him save you from worry, addiction, debt, sickness, and emotional pain. Every promise in the Book belongs to you. Don't wait to receive His great salvation.

Once made perfect, [Christ] became the source
of eternal salvation for all who obey him.

HEBREWS 5:9

You are truly the perfect woman. Others may bring up your past or point out your mistakes, but God has made you perfect through Christ Jesus. Your old life is passed away and all things are new. You have a fresh start—a clean slate. God doesn't remember the old you. Every sin has been forgotten in His mind. Forget it in yours. It's a new day with new dreams. You have been given a whole new life. Start living it!

Satisfaction

"I will refresh the weary and satisfy the faint."
JEREMIAH 31:25

Satisfaction is the result of a job well done. Sometimes your expectation for the blessings of God requires you to press a little harder and stretch your faith a little farther to see the results you've asked God for. You can be sure all your effort will be rewarded. God promises to satisfy your soul—a deep satisfaction only He can provide. He's given you the power to reach your destiny. He will not let you fail. Press on! Press on!

[The Lord] satisfies me with good things
and makes me young again, like the eagle.

PSALM 103:5 NCV

The enormous wealth of love God has for you compels Him to shower you with His presence and draw you close to Him. The fresh scent that remains after a spring rain shower is an open invitation to rest in His mercy and grace. The flutter of a hummingbird's wings or the gentle sigh from a toddler's crib sends a special message that expresses His gentle desire to satisfy your heart with everything good.

Security

The righteous will never be moved. . . .
Their hearts are firm, secure in the LORD.

PSALM 112:6–7 NRSV

God is your safe haven from all of life's difficulty. When the pressures of life seem more than you can take—grab hold of the stability found only in Him. You're His for safekeeping. He stands ready to receive you with open arms. The blanket of His love and compassion are there to surround you and bring warmth to your heart during life's coldest hours. Stand under His umbrella of protection throughout the storms. Take refuge in Him—He's your sanctuary!

*Trust in the LORD, and do good; so you will
live in the land, and enjoy security.*

PSALM 37:3 NRSV

Throughout history the church building served as a place of sanctuary for criminals and debtors to escape the wrath of those who wanted to pay them back for wrongs done. They could not be touched until they had received due process and were found guilty for their crimes. Jesus offers you asylum in much the same way. He has even paid the penalty for your crimes. His righteousness given to you is your safe place.

Self-Control

Prepare your minds for action; be self-controlled;
set your hope fully on the grace to be given
you when Jesus Christ is revealed.

1 PETER 1:13

There are moments in every woman's life when her emotions take on a life of their own. When those times come to your life, God wants you to walk by faith and not by sight—being led by confidence in Him rather than your feelings. The gift of self-control will put you in His best light and keep you from responding foolishly. He stands ready to help you choose self-control. Believe in Him, because He believes in you.

Let us be self-controlled, putting on faith and love as a breastplate, and the hope of salvation as a helmet.

1 THESSALONIANS 5:8

Self-control is the ability to control your own behavior, especially your reactions and impulses. You alone are responsible for your choices, decisions, and actions. God has given you the Holy Spirit to help you live as you were designed to live—a productive, fulfilled life. No matter what others do or say, you have the power to do what is right. God has given you all the tools you need to come out on top.

Serving God

"Acknowledge the God of your father, and serve him with wholehearted devotion and with a willing mind, for the LORD searches every heart and understands every motive behind the thoughts."

1 CHRONICLES 28:9

Perhaps God didn't call you to be a missionary or preach the Gospel, yet you are still called to serve God, and it's much easier than you think. It's simply allowing God in you to do what He's equipped you to do. If you like to talk, you may be an encourager. If you like to bake, perhaps you have the gift of hospitality. Inside you there are blessings for others waiting to be handed out. You're serving God day after day—exactly the way He intended.

"Whoever serves me must follow me;
and where I am, my servant also will be.
My Father will honor the one who serves me."

JOHN 12:26

Serving God has no limits. Today women can serve God in any way they desire. No calling is too big or too small. Perhaps you're raising the next generation—your own children—to serve God. Maybe you speak to hundreds of thousands through books or on public platforms. Let your faith soar and remove anything that limits you. As you follow God, He will make the impossible possible. When you think you can, you can.

Singleness

When you're unmarried, you're free to
concentrate on simply pleasing the Master.
1 Corinthians 7:32 MSG

There is a season for everything on earth—that includes your singleness. Whether you remain single throughout your life or choose one day to marry, this is a special time, a time when you are free to grow and learn and draw closer to God. Singleness is full of treasures. Many singles miss these because they are focused on the future. Rejoice in the now. See what God has in store for you today.

God gives the gift of the single life to some,
the gift of the married life to others.

1 Corinthians 7:7 msg

Society can add great pressure to conform to the norm of married life. Take courage in who you are today. God has great plans for you now—not just in the future! He's not waiting on you to get married to fulfill your destiny. Your plan and purpose in life is about YOU! You can boldly live for Him today and trust Him to take care of tomorrow. He's given you everything you need to live a great life. What are you waiting for?

Sleep

I will lie down and sleep in peace, for you alone,
O LORD, make me dwell in safety.

PSALM 4:8

Strangely, your body was designed like a battery. It runs down and has to be recharged. That's why sleep is so important. Your body powers down and reaches a point in which you are fully relaxed. Then you begin to refuel and rebuild. It's a time of restoration for your body and your mind. The Lord has promised you the blessing of peaceful sleep. You can relax and take comfort knowing He never sleeps but watches over you at all times.

I lie down and sleep; I wake again,
for the LORD sustains me.

PSALM 3:5 NRSV

Fear is the opposite of faith. Sometimes it comes disguised as worry or despair, and very often it tries to rob you of precious sleep. The Bible says love casts out all fear and faith works by love. As you fall asleep, think of just how much God loves you. Build your faith by recalling all He has done for you. Count your blessings instead of sheep; then sleep peacefully in your heavenly Father's protective arms.

Speech

A [woman] finds joy in giving an apt reply—
and how good is a timely word!

PROVERBS 15:23

Your life experiences speak of God's faithfulness and love, and He wants you to share what He's done for you with others. Someone out there may be struggling to take the next step toward God's love and plan for her life, and you can bring encouragement by sharing how God helped you through the tough times. In the process, your own faith will be strengthened. You have answers. Be bold and courageous. Speak up!

Gracious speech is like clover honey—
good taste to the soul, quick energy for the body.

PROVERBS 16:24 MSG

Women are quoted throughout the history books for their inspirational speeches and clever wisdom that helped a community, a city, or a nation overcome crisis. At the time they were just sharing a word of encouragement. That same God who inspired them lives inside of you. You can be inspiration to your family, friends, and coworkers. You can provide substance for the souls of those around you. Your words have power.

Spiritual Growth

We, who with unveiled faces all reflect the Lord's glory, are being transformed into his likeness with ever-increasing glory, which comes from the Lord, who is the Spirit.

2 CORINTHIANS 3:18

Each day, whether you know it or not, you are growing in the Lord, becoming more and more like Him. Simply because His Spirit dwells within you, you are being transformed from the inside out, reflecting the glory of God that burns from within. That's why you will often feel a nudge from deep down inside to deal with a certain issue or let go of a negative thought or behavior. You are literally growing up in God. How wonderful is that!

This is my prayer: that your love may abound
more and more in knowledge and depth of insight.

PHILIPPIANS 1:9

The Spirit of God works within you to transform you to His image, but you must do your part, as well. Your job is to respond to the work being done inside. You must relinquish sin, build up your spirit by reading God's Word, open your heart to wisdom and counsel, and surrender your old nature to be replaced by your new one. Your spiritual growth is intended to be a collaboration between you and God. The work is often difficult, but it brings great rewards.

Strength

The Lord is my strength, my song, and my salvation.
He is my God, and I will praise him.

EXODUS 15:2 TLB

In the universe, there is really just one source of strength—that is God. Others may be strong for you, on your behalf, but they cannot impart that strength to you. When you invite God to fill your heart and life, you are strengthened from within. His strength literally becomes your strength. You are empowered to do, to stand, to fight, to conquer. If Christ is there, you don't need to reach outside yourself for strength. Reach inside and find all you need.

I can do everything through him
who gives me strength.

PHILIPPIANS 4:13

You're probably busier than you've ever been—doing more than you've ever done. Maybe you feel exhausted—physically, mentally, and emotionally. God has given you strength for your days—even the toughest ones. He is the source you can draw on when you feel your supply is running low. You don't have to go at life alone. When you reach for Him, He's always there, ready to refresh you. Find quiet moments to dip your soul into His supply. You'll come away strengthened and renewed.

Success

Wisdom brings success.
ECCLESIASTES 10:10 NKJV

God has great plans for you. Sometimes your own plans may sound more adventurous or even more profitable than what God has for you. But remember, He sees and knows all—the beginning from the end. He knows the best road to take to get you to your destiny. He sees the obstacles along the way. He sees the eternal as well as the physical. Embrace the future He has for you, and you'll be a true success story.

*[It is not that] we think we can do anything
of lasting value by ourselves. Our only power
and success comes from God.*

2 CORINTHIANS 3:5 TLB

God created you for success, but He never planned for you to acquire it alone. You may experience a small measure of success here and there by your own wit, but imagine where you can go in God. True success comes when you're willing to say, "It's not about me and all about You, Lord." Then He is free to take you to a level that you can only achieve with His strength and power propelling you. Then you'll discover lasting success in Him.

Thankfulness

Give thanks to the LORD, for he is good;
his love endures forever.

1 Chronicles 16:34

Each of the four seasons—fall, winter, spring, and summer—demonstrate creation's thankfulness to God for a job well done. The trees bow before heaven as their leaves fall gracefully to the ground. The glistening snowfall speaks of God's majesty. Flowers of every kind bow low to the glory of God in spring, and summer warms to the glow of all the blessings God has to offer. What has God done for you? Take a moment and express your gratefulness to Him in your own way.

Thanks be to God, which giveth us the victory through our Lord Jesus Christ.

1 Corinthians 15:57 KJV

What a wonderful, giving God we serve. He stands with an extended hand, ready to give you the desires of your heart. Take a moment to offer thanks to Him for the greatest gifts, the awesome joys you've experienced, and even the small things that you realize He engineered to bless you in an unexpected way. Share with Him just how much He means to you. Express to Him your thankfulness. He is worthy of your thanks.

Thoughts

When my anxious thoughts multiply within me,
Your consolations delight my soul.

PSALM 94:19 NASB

Your thoughts produce your attitudes and behaviors—your actions. They are, of all your physical assets, the most powerful. Your heavenly Father wants you to direct your thoughts toward life and blessing. The Bible says to think about those things that are pure, honest, true, virtuous, lovely, and of a good report. When you control your thoughts, they cannot be used by the enemy of your soul to harass you. Your thoughts will help you become free in every aspect of your life.

*We take captive every thought to make
it obedient to Christ.*

2 CORINTHIANS 10:5

God gave you a creative mind filled with an amazing
ability to think and reason. Your thoughts are the starting
point of every decision you make and action you take. Your
loving heavenly Father gave you guidelines in His Word
to help you determine the direction your thoughts should
take. He created you to fulfill every dream He placed inside
you. Think higher—His way of thinking produces peace,
health, prosperity, wisdom, and so many blessings.

Trust

Trust the LORD with all your heart,
and don't depend on your own understanding.

PROVERBS 3:5 NCV

Teammates have to rely on one another to succeed in any endeavor. They have to have a certain level of confidence in one another and their abilities to help them succeed. God trusts you enough to put you on His eternal team. He has confidence in you because He knows you can do all things through Christ, who gives you strength. He chose you to stand alongside your team captain, Jesus, and go to the board for a win!

*"Anyone who trusts in [God] will
never be put to shame."*

ROMANS 10:11

As you look back on the journey you've traveled, recall the times you placed hope and confidence in God. The outcome might not have been exactly as you imagined, but God is always faithful to bring you through. Count each blessing He's given you along the way and consider them stepping-stones to a higher level of trust. Whatever you're facing today, you can rest assured that His blessings will never stop. He will walk it out with you—every step of the way.

Truth

*Speaking the truth in love. . .grow up into him
in all things, which is the head, even Christ.*

EPHESIANS 4:15 KJV

Heated words really stress relationships. A white lie
may seem more easily swallowed than the blunt truth of
a situation, but God has blessed you with the help of His
Holy Spirit to bring truth into the lives of others. He knows
their hearts and the words that should be spoken to bring
them closer to God and to you. Truth mixed with love is a
rich treasure, and when it overflows out of your heart, it
becomes a beautiful gift to those around you.

*"You shall know the truth, and the truth
shall make you free."*

JOHN 8:32 NKJV

Jesus is Truth. Like 24 karat gold is pure gold—without impurities—Jesus is pure truth. The light and life of God lives in you; therefore, the blessing of truth is always available to you, helping you know and discern what is good and right for your life. Jesus never promised your pathway would be easy, but He has promised to never leave you. Truth is always with you. And you can call upon Him in every circumstance to light your way.

Waiting

Be strong, and let your heart take courage,
all you who wait for the LORD.

PSALM 31:24 NRSV

God waits for you. You are the precious fruit of the earth, and like a farmer waits for harvest, God is waiting for you. Imagine what it must be like for Him to wait for you to grow, building trust and confidence in Him. He offers you spiritual food and water, believing you will take root and become strong and confident in His Word and in your relationship with Him. And to Him, you're well worth the wait.

If we hope for what we do not see,
we wait for it with patience.

ROMANS 8:25 NRSV

Waiting eventually produces blessing after a time of transition. Consider a woman in labor awaiting the birth of her baby. She's not sitting still—she's experiencing active labor. She's working hard through transition. How exciting to know that what you've asked God for is on its way. As God works behind the scenes to bring about everything you're waiting for, your faith is at work preparing for the arrival of His blessing.

Wholeness

The very God of peace sanctify you wholly;
and I pray God your whole spirit and soul
and body be preserved blameless unto
the coming of our Lord Jesus Christ.

1 THESSALONIANS 5:23 KJV

Human beings—and especially women—are uniquely complex. Emotions of the soul play on attitudes of the mind and together impact the body, which responds with intensity enough to affect emotions and establish attitudes. That's why it's important to be wholly surrendered to God. You must nurture and nourish every aspect of who you are. Ask God to establish harmony in your life, mind, and soul conformed to God's ways and a body that reflects inner peace.

[Jesus] said unto him, Arise, go thy way:
thy faith hath made thee whole.

LUKE 17:19 KJV

Wholeness is a faith matter—not necessarily faith that God is going to touch you right here, right now, but faith that wholeness of spirit, mind, and body will come as you surrender all aspects of yourself to Him and begin to serve Him. God rarely removes our limitations before we start down the path. Instead, they fall into the background as we get on our way. Ask God to make you whole—completely whole—and then begin living your life to the full.

Wisdom

The Lord gives wisdom; from his mouth come
knowledge and understanding.

PROVERBS 2:6 NRSV

Have you ever had that feeling deep in your gut that you should—or shouldn't—do something? The Holy Spirit dwells within you, ready to give you the wisdom you need to make good choices for your life. If you're listening, you will hear Him, but He is a gentleman. He won't shout or force you to hear what He has to say. The more you trust His lead, the more you will grow in wisdom.

The fear of the LORD is the beginning of wisdom;
all who follow his precepts have good
understanding. To him belongs eternal praise.

PSALM 111:10

When you find yourself in a jam, you don't have to figure it out on your own. God has answers to the questions you ask. You may find wisdom in a scripture that He prompts you to read, an insight in conversation with a friend. You need His wisdom every single day. God stands ready to assist. All you have to do is ask Him for help and then listen for the answer. Be encouraged—God has all the answers you need.

Work

The desires of the diligent
are fully satisfied.

PROVERBS 13:4

Regardless of whether your work is in an office or in your home or in your home office, each morning when you open your eyes, you've got a job to do. God is pleased when you apply yourself diligently to the task He's given you. It may be pleasant work—it may not. Whatever it is, see it as your gift to your heavenly Father for the day. Do it as if He were watching your every step—because He is.

Bible Permissions

Scripture Index

OLD TESTAMENT

1 Kings
8:61...48

2 Kings
18:32...44

1 Chronicles
16:34...194
28:9...180
29:17...118

2 Chronicles
15:7...64

Psalms
3:3...56
3:5...185
4:8...184
5:3...74
9:1–2...145
10:17...68
19:1...136
25:9...38